The Indians of Canada /A Survey

Edward S. Rogers/Curator of Ethnology
The Royal Ontario Museum

'The Indians of Canada — A Survey', one in a series of six introductory guides to the Indians of Canada, is produced by the Royal Ontario Museum in association with the National Film Board of Canada.
A film strip, "The Indians of Canada: a Survey" to accompany this guide may be obtained from the National Film Board of Canada, P.O. Box 6100, Montreal 3.

RŌM

How do we know the Indians' past?

Archaeology and Ethnohistory are two
means by which information is secured about
the Indians' past. Archaeology is a technique
for gaining information from the ground,
through the excavation of homes, burials
and temple sites in which stone and bone
tools, pottery and any other non-perishable
items have been preserved. Unfortunately,
much of a people's culture, such as their
social organization, their values and religious
systems, has not been preserved, although
parts may be inferred from the material
remains.

Basically, material is retrieved from the
ground through controlled excavations using
shovels and, for fine work, trowels and
brushes so that no object is damaged. First,
the site is mapped, and then squares are
laid out, marked by a post at each corner.
Then the site is excavated, square by square.
The different soil layers and artifacts they
contain are removed from the top to the
bottom layer, the last being the oldest. As
each specimen is discovered, its exact
position is noted in relation to one of the
corner posts, its depth below the surface and
the soil layer in which it was found.

Once specimens such as potsherds or
arrowheads have been removed from the
ground, it is necessary to date and interpret
them. From all of the materials excavated
it is possible to give some ideas as to the way
of life of the people who once lived at that
particular site. Much time has necessarily
been devoted to the establishment of classifications and of dating sequences before it
becomes possible to make further inferences
regarding the way of life of the people.

Ethnohistory deals with the Indians' past
only since the time of written records. These
are examined for information regarding the
life of the Indians at different times, from
which a picture of their history and culture
may be gained.

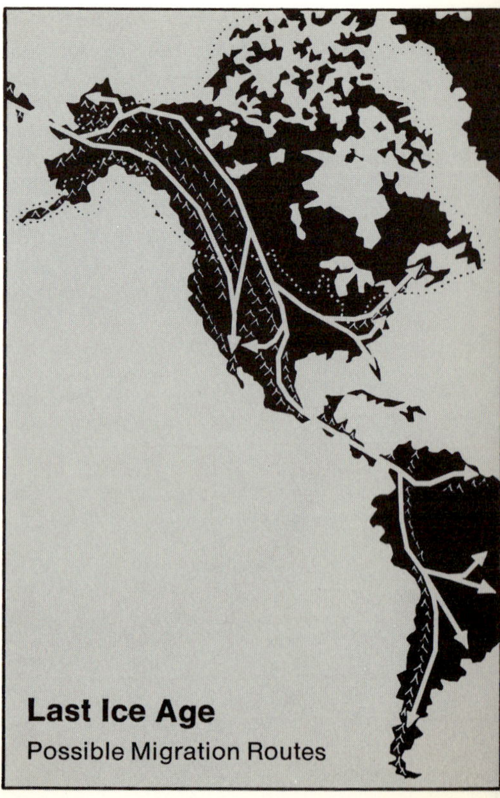

Man's Entry into the New World

is generally agreed that man entered the New World from Northeastern Asia by crossing Bering Strait. Depending on the time of entry, estimated at between 20,000 and 40,000 years ago, he may have crossed on a land bridge, by boat or over the ice to Beringia — present-day Alaska. Ice may have blocked further advance but in time it melted and man then moved south. Presumably at first he migrated southward on the east side of the Rocky Mountains, spreading from there throughout North America. The movement may have been quite rapid since environmental conditions were much the same along his route. From North America man moved on into Central America and finally penetrated South America as far as Tierra del Fuego. There may have been, at a later date, occasional contact across the Pacific Ocean.

It has been suggested that there were two major waves of migrants into North America: the original colonizers who came during the Ice Age and remained in Beringia (Alaska)

for a time and, at a much more recent date, a second wave. The former multiplied, spread out and populated both North and South America; the latter are thought to have been the ancestors of the Athapaskans of northern North America. Typical Eskimo culture is now thought to have developed within the area of Beringia and not to have been derived from Asia.

The migrants, both the first and later arrivals, were all representatives of modern man, *Homo sapiens.* Man did not evolve in the New World, but rather somewhere in the Old World.

The first Canadians came as hunters of big game animals. They had, no doubt, the ability to make fire, to chip stone tools such as spear points and knives and to work bone. Presumably, they had some form of shelter and clothing. Their social organization was most likely based on ties of kinship. Studies of recent hunters (ethnography) suggest that the migrants must have had some concept of supernatural powers and performed certain rituals connected with the hunting of game animals.

Early Man in the New World

Although it is thought that man has been present in the New World for 20,000 to 40,000 years, the first proven date is approximately 10,000 years old. The period before this date, extending back perhaps to 40,000 B.C., is known as the *pre-Projectile Point Horizon.* Very little is known of the people's way of life. When man entered the New World, he had to make a number of adaptations to environments as different as those of the Arctic Coast of Bering Strait, the tropical areas of Central and South America, and the Subarctic regions of Tierra del Fuego at the southern tip of South America. These various adaptations were made during many centuries elapsing between man's first crossing of Bering Strait and his final settlement at the extreme southern tip of the New World.

By 10,000 years ago, there were two main cultural adaptations in North America. One, the *Big Game Hunting Tradition* (Clovis, Folsom and Sandia peoples), extended from the Plains to the Atlantic coast and south of the Ice Sheet that then spread over much of Canada. Much of the country was lush grasslands with trees along the streams. In the east there were deciduous forests. The people hunted big game — mammoth, camel, horse, a large species of bison and the giant sloth. Most likely, smaller game was taken whenever possible and there was some gathering of nuts, berries and roots. Some of the animals are now extinct, perhaps killed off by early man.

The Old Cordillerian Tradition, the second cultural adaptation, existed about the same time as the Big Game Hunting Tradition, but was located in Western North America. It was an unspecialized hunting, fishing and collecting culture using projectile points, bolas, small gravers and crude choppers.

Between 8,000 and 5,000 B.C., the environment changed toward modern conditions. At the same time, new cultural traditions developed — modifications of the old — by which the people could exploit the new conditions. Four main traditions arose, two of which might be mentioned.

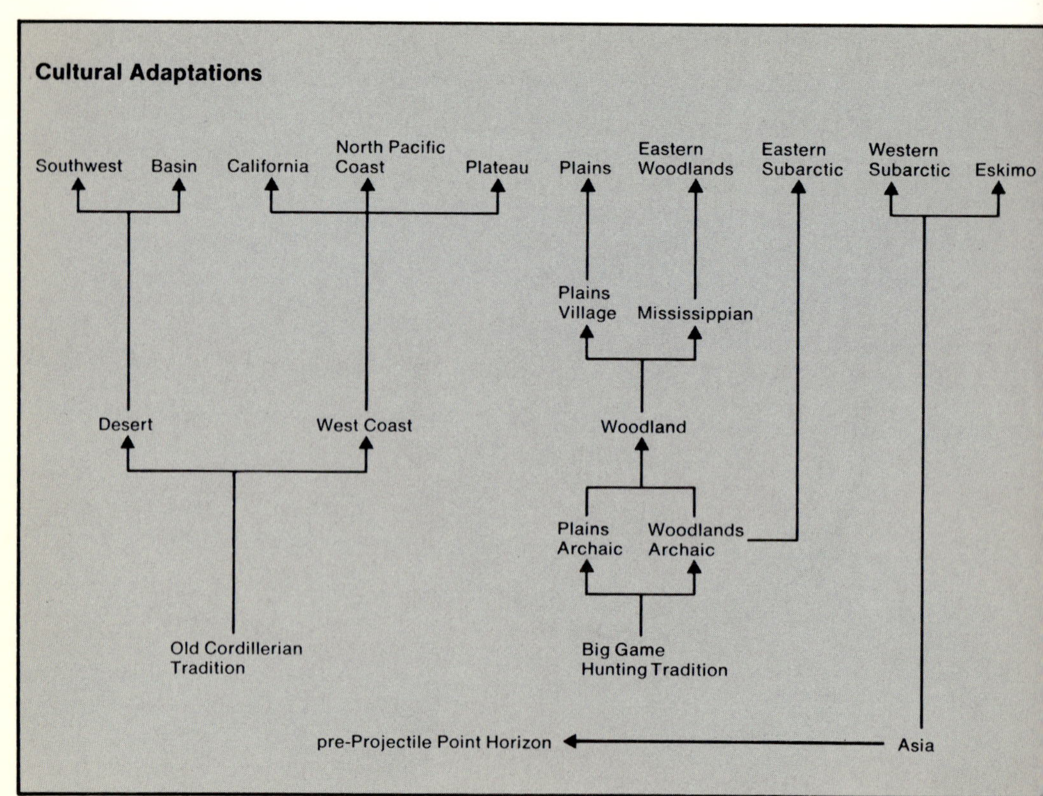

In eastern North America the people hunted small game — deer, raccoon, opossum and birds — fished and collected not only plants but mussels. Later a greater reliance was placed on collecting; numbers of milling stones have been found. Eventually, the people began to cultivate plants such as sunflower and artichoke. It was at this time that ground stone tools were first made. Since the people raised a few crops, they led a more sedentary existence.

In the west, a different way of life was evolving. The people were constantly on the move in search of animals and ripening plants. Much dependence was placed on wild plant foods: acorns, pinon nuts, grass seeds, bulbs, berries and roots. Many of these were prepared with grinding stones. The peoples hunted modern species of mountain sheep, bison, deer, antelope and small game for meat and hides. Possessions were few. The social organization was based on small family units.

Between 5,000 B.C. and the arrival of the Europeans, a number of specialized cultures arose from the preceding traditions. These are referred to as Culture Areas, based on the way in which each group of Indians lived.

The Rise of Complex Societies in the New World

The Indian inhabitants of the New World made many notable advances and achievements. Many developed complex societies. These were found from the southeastern United States through Mexico, Central America and into the Andes of Peru. Perha, the most spectacular were the Aztec, Maya and Inca Empires, true states with strong central political organization dominated by a priesthood. Wars of conquest were under taken to form these empires. The people bu large cities and were skilled stone-masons, constructing temples and other structures. The Inca erected stone walls, of enormous rocks, cut to fit so tightly that a knife blade could not be inserted between two blocks.

The basis on which these empires arose wa agriculture. Farm work was by hand since t Indians had no domesticated animals, such horses or oxen, of sufficient strength to draw ploughs.

By approximately 7,000 B.C., these Indians were raising pumpkins, by 6,000 B.C. squas and by 5,000 B.C. maize. By the time of Christ, maize was being cultivated from southern Canada to northwestern Argentina In addition to these three basic crops, vario varieties of beans, pineapple, guava, white potato, sweet potato, peanut, artichokes, yam, bottle gourds, tomatoes, avacados, chile peppers and tobacco were grown. Cotton was domesticated by 1,700 B.C.

Not only were the Indians remarkable for their agricultural skills, but they also developed a number of concepts which were as refined as any to be found in the world at the time. The Maya, for example, invented the zero for use with a sophisticated mathematics equal to systems in use in Babylonia, India and China. Writing, which was both pictographic and phonetic, was also a Maya invention. For writing, they made good paper of *amatl* bark. Furthermore, their astronomical knowledge and methods of reckoning time were highly accurate. The Incas had developed extremely intricate techniques for weaving cotton. In fact, some of their techniques cannot be duplicated today with modern machinery. Metal work in gold and silver was of the finest quality, especially for delicate ornaments, cast by the "lost wax" process. The Indians in the area of advanced civilizations were skilful in working stone. Even the hardest stone, quartz, was not too difficult for their carvers. Furthermore, they were skilled potters.

The European Arrives

The first Europeans to arrive were the Vikings who came from Greenland in 1,000 A.D. They did not, however, make any permanent settlements in the New World. It is thought they explored the Labrador Coast as far south as Newfoundland and perhaps beyond. A site has been excavated at L'Anse au Meadow, Newfoundland, which may have been a Viking iron foundry; it has been dated around 1,000 A.D.

The next to arrive were the Spaniards when, in 1492, Columbus entered the Caribbean. The Spanish invaded Mexico, moving south to Peru and north into California massacring and despoiling the Indians. It was Coronado who in 1541 first saw and described the Plains Indians.

To the north, Europeans were exploring and exploiting the St. Lawrence River Valley. Basques, Portuguese and Bretons were fishing in the Gulf of the St. Lawrence by the first decade of the 16th century and perhaps earlier. In 1534, Cartier sailed up the St. Lawrence as far as what is today Montreal but was stopped by the Lachine Rapids. The French returned again, and in the early 1600s Champlain made a permanent settlement at Quebec. The French then explored west up the Ottawa River. In the mid-1600s Radisson and Groseilliers explored the Great Lakes; in the 1740s La Vérendrye pushed out onto the Canadian Plains.

Meanwhile, the English were settling between the French to the north and the Spanish to the south and they soon began moving west. In 1763 the British acquired all of Canada. By the end of the century Alexander Mackenzie had followed the Mackenzie River to the Arctic Ocean and later travelled over the Rockies to the Pacific Coast. The Pacific Coast had already been explored by Vancouver and Cook of the British navy. In 1804 Lewis and Clark began their westward journey up the Missouri and down the Clearwater River to the Columbia and on to the Pacific Ocean. By now the greater portion of North America had been traversed although most remained without settlements. Furthermore, a picture of the various Indian groups who once were the owners of the continent was vaguely known.

What did the Europeans find?

The Europeans as they explored North America found Indians living practically everywhere, peoples possessed of a variety of cultures and many languages. This was an age in which Europeans were curious about the world and its inhabitants. Captured Indians and items of their manufacture were taken back to the courts of Europe as curiosities. These collections of artifacts often were the basis on which museums later arose. The Indians also had an impact on contemporary philosophers and writers, such as Rousseau, Pope and Swift. Since the Indians' origin was not accounted for in the Bible, the Indian stimulated great interest. Early attempts were made to discover something of his background. As early as the late 1700s, President Thomas Jefferson, out of curiosity as to Indian history, excavated a mound near his home in Virginia, one of the first archaeological endeavours.

Besides collecting specimens and capturing Indians, many of the early explorers wrote accounts of what they saw and were told. One of the most complete and earliest is that of Sagard, written in 1623-4, published in 1632, describing the Huron Indians. This can be considered one of the "first" ethnographies of any group of Canadian Indians. The Jesuit missionaries wrote at length about the Indians, primarly the Algonkians and Iroquoians.

Attempts were made to organize the bewildering array of information from these and later accounts describing the diversities of languages and cultures of the American Indians. During the middle of the last century, John Wesley Powell, for the United States government, worked out a classification of the major languages spoken in the United States, from which later and more refined classifications have been made. At the turn of the century, Clark Wissler, under the influence of Franz Boas, developed the concept of the "Culture Area" when arranging the ethnological displays at the Chicago Exhibition of 1892. Each area included those tribes who had quite similar ways of life and from this a generalized account could be made of the culture of the area.

Six major culture areas are represented in Canada — the *Arctic, North Pacific Coast, Plateau, Subarctic, Plains* and *Eastern Woodlands*. In this series neither the Arctic nor Plateau Culture Areas are described.

Synopsis of Culture Areas of Canada

The *North Pacific Coast Culture Area,* a sea-coast environment, extended from northern California to the panhandle of Alaska. The coast is indented with many fiords and backed by high mountains. Rainfall is heavy, and the climate mild. Forest growth is dense and consists of huge trees such as the cedars. Mammals included deer, bear, mountain goat and sheep, wolves and smaller fur bearers. Fish were abundant — salmon in the rivers and cod and halibut in the ocean.

The North Pacific Coast Indians lived mainly by fishing and some hunting. Plentiful food — fish from the rivers and oceans — encouraged a relatively dense and settled population. Salmon were the principal catch, taken in the spring and early summer; the fish were smoked and dried for winter use. Halibut, cod, candle fish (or eulachon), occasionally seals, whale that drifted on shore and shell fish provided additional food.

Their technology was designed for wood working. Wood, especially cedar, was the k item in the manufacture of much of their material equipment — boxes, large dugout canoes, planking for their houses, totem poles and other carved posts, bowls, dishes and ladles. Wood-working tools consisted o adzes, knives, chisels, mauls, wedges, and awls. Cedar bark was used for making rain-capes and mats; spruce roots for hats. They also wove blankets of mountain goat and dc hair. Trade was important both up and dowr the coast and inland along the "grease trails," so named because quantities of eulachon oil were carried along these trails.

With food easily obtained locally, the people lived the year round in villages. Each village was placed on a beach at the head o a sheltered bay and consisted of several multi-family plank houses which faced the sea. Each village was generally independen of all others, although at times several might join together to make war on some other group. The village was under the leadership of a chief and each dwelling had its own house-chief.

The people were organized into clans which in the north were matrilineal (recognizing descent through the women) and in the south tended to be patrilineal (recognizing descen through the men). There was basically a three-class system — Nobles, Commoners and Slaves, the latter usually taken in war. The Nobles or Chiefs were the political head and the leaders at the potlatch (a large ceremonial feast).

Since sufficient food could be secured durin the spring and summer to last the rest of the year, the winter months were a time of leisure. Then great ceremonies were enactec and the potlatch or large ritual feast held. The potlatch was of extreme importance. An individual, even though of noble birth, could not inherit a position without having first given a potlatch or having it performed for him by a father or uncle. At a potlatch, gifts were given away in order to validate his new title, his right to the myths that he might recount and the songs that he might sing.

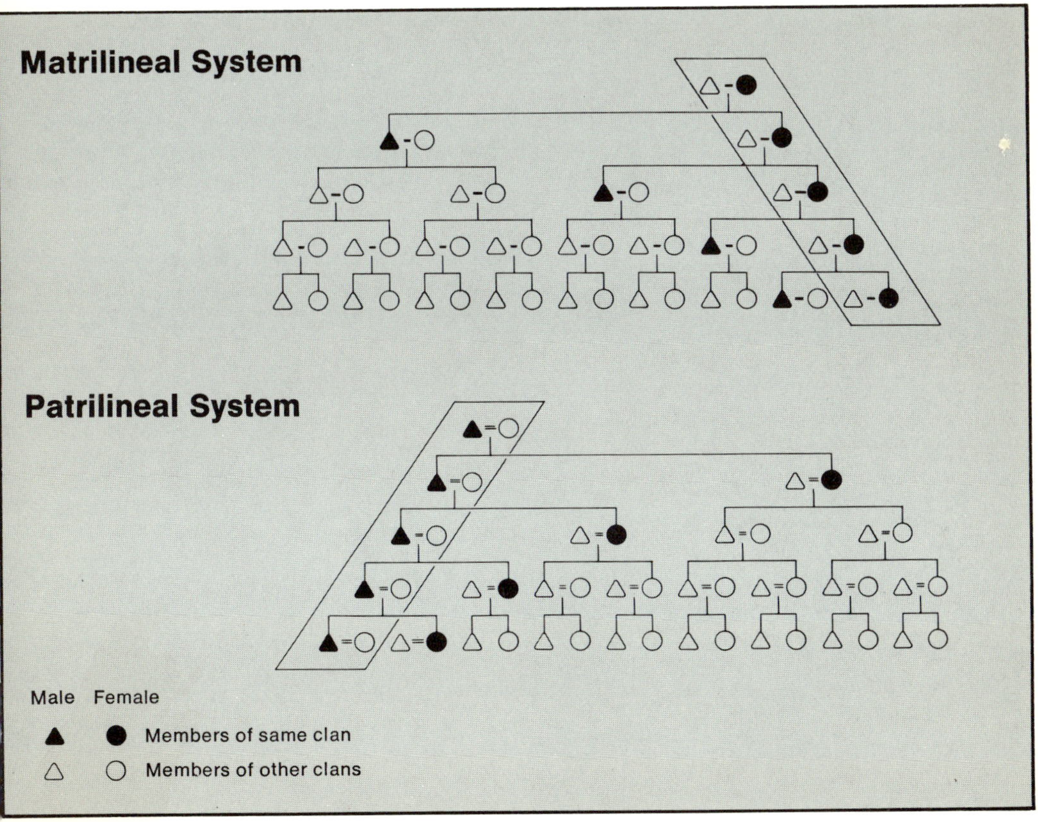

Matrilineal System

Patrilineal System

Male   Female

▲   ●   Members of same clan

△   ○   Members of other clans

The *Subarctic Culture Area* was enormous, reaching from the Labrador coast across Canada and Alaska to the mouth of the Yukon River. Except in the west where it impinged upon the Rocky Mountains, it was a land of low lying relief covered with boreal forest composed mainly of conifers. Winters were long and cold with extremes of sub-zero weather. Summers were short and relatively mild. Within this region lived moose, caribou, black bear, beaver and a number of smaller mammals, as well as waterfowl and grouse. In the many streams and lakes were trout, whitefish, pike and suckers.

The Indians of the Subarctic lived by hunting and fishing. Big game, the principal form sought, was not sufficient to provide them with all they needed and of necessity they had to secure, whenever possible, smaller game, birds, and fish. Much of the year was spent in searching for something to eat.

Subarctic technology was relatively simple and yet effective in coping with the environment. Since the people were almost constantly on the move, material possessions were limited, and housing was such that it could be transported easily or made of readily available materials. Canoes were essential for mobility in summer when overland transportation was difficult or impossible, especially in the Eastern Subarctic. Snowshoes and toboggans were the two means of winter travel when snow covered the ground.

It was a culture in which the working of bark, hide and wood was important. Bark was used for lodge and canoe coverings and containers. Wood was used in the manufacture of canoe and snowshoe frames, toboggans, paddles, dishes and the framework of lodges. Hide was used for clothing, lodge coverings and containers and, cut into strips, for the lacing of snowshoes and tying together toboggans.

There were no settled villages among the Subarctic Indians. Rather there were summer encampments of perhaps a hundred Indians situated at good fishing sites. With the advent of fall, the group broke up into hunting groups that scattered in search of food, not to reunite again, as a rule, until the following spring. There were no powerful political leaders. An elder, respected for his wisdom and religious knowledge, might be consulted during the summer at the settlement. During the winter the leader of the hunting group, the oldest man with the most religious knowledge, determined where the group would go and when.

Warfare was limited since there was little leisure time. There was, however, a limited amount of trade between various groups within the Subarctic and with neighbouring areas.

The religious philosophy, but not the ritual paraphernalia, of the people was highly developed even though so much time had to be spent in simple survival. It was in large measure oriented to the food quest. The bear, the beaver and the caribou were of extreme ritual importance.

The *Plains Culture Area* extended from central Alberta and Saskatchewan, south to the Gulf of Mexico, west to the foot of the Rockies and east roughly to the Mississippi River. The plains are a flat land several thousand feet in elevation. Here and there rivers have cut valleys eastward from the foothils of the Rockies to the Mississippi. The land was covered by tall grass in the east and short grass in the west. Trees were only found along the river banks and in the foot-hills of the Rockies. Also found were antelope and, in the foothills, elk and deer. It was the home of the coyote, prairie dog and badger. Fish were few and of no importance to the Indians of the Plains except those in the north.

To the Indians of the plains, the bison was the basis of life. Its flesh furnished them with food, its hide with lodge coverings, shields and moccasin soles, its sinew with thread, and its bones with tools. Its skull was a ritual object in the Sun Dance. Other game was taken, roots were dug and berries collected.

The technology possessed by the Plains Indians was not complex, but rather consisted of basic tools: mauls, knives, scrapers, fleshers and awls. Much of the tool kit was adapted to the processing of bison. Wood-working was limited and there was no weaving or use of bark. The people lived in large tipis covered with bison hides.The poles for the foundation were often secured in the foothills of the Rockies. Dogs were used to carry packs and drag travois. Later, when the Indians had acquired horses these were used for transporting goods, dragging travois and for riding. Clothing was of hide, usually of deer or elk skins decorated originally with porcupine quills. After the advent of traders, beadwork became exceedingly prominent in ornamenting clothing and personal equipment.

During the summer, the bands that were members of a particular tribe gathered together on the high plains for the bison hunt. The lodges were erected in a camp circle with the entrance facing east. In the centre of the circle was the council lodge where the chiefs met to decide the policy of the hunt. They were aided by a "society of soldiers" who prevented anyone from prematurely hunting bison. Once the decision was made all the men joined in the hunt. Afterwards, the women butchered the game, dressed the hides and prepared the meat. At the end of summer, the large tribal group broke up into bands of a few hundred people each, who then moved back into sheltered valleys or the foothills of the Rockies to spend the winter protected from the cold winds that swept across the plains. In spring all the bands again joined together.

Warfare was important to the Plains Indians. Through warfare a man gained prestige. It was not carried out to gain territory or to kill one's enemies. Rather it was a daring exploit to steal horses from within the centre of the camp circle and get away unharmed, or to touch an enemy in battle and escape without killing him. In this way a man could count *coup* and elevate himself in the eyes of the rest of the people.

A certain amount of trade existed between neighbouring groups. Obsidian used for arrowheads was secured from the Yellowstone River country and catlinite for pipes was secured from Minnesota. Through capture, horses went from group to group.

Plains Indians were an extremely religious people and their main ceremony, the Sun Dance, was held at the tribal gathering during the summer. If an individual faced misfortune he might vow to hold the Sun Dance the following summer, in this way hoping to gain the blessings of the spirits to help him overcome his troubles. When the time came, those who knew the ritual would coach him and any others who were to participate in the ceremony.

The *Eastern Woodland Culture Area* extended from west of the Great Lakes east to the Atlantic. The country was hilly and rolling, dotted here and there with lakes and ponds joined by streams and rivers. The winters were cold but not too long and the summers could be quite warm. The area was covered with deciduous forests of oak, beech, maple and elm. In addition, there were stands of pine and spruce. Inhabiting the forest were deer, elk, bear, beaver, porcupine, raccoon and other smaller fur-bearers. Also encountered were ducks, passenger pigeons and grouse, as well as many song birds. The streams and lakes held fish such as pike, bass, perch and trout.

The Indians lived in a variety of ways. There was hunting, especially of deer. There was fishing, some spots being extremely rich; at Sault Ste Marie, Ontario, large quantities of whitefish were secured in the rapids every fall. In addition, berries and other vegetal products were gathered, especially wild rice in the Minnesota-Wisconsin region. Furthermore, agriculture was practised, corn, beans and squash being raised.

The technology of the Indians of the Eastern Woodlands was relatively simple. They possessed hoes for agricultural purposes, and mortars and pestles for preparing maize. They had adzes and crooked knives for working wood. To produce splint baskets they had splint cutters and, to prepare hides, scrapers of bone. Formerly, they manufactured pottery but with the advent of Europeans, they secured metal containers. In the western part of the area, the Indians secured wool from bison from which they wove bags, belts, garters and scarves. In addition, they used rushes and corn husks to weave mats.

Those Indians who actively engaged in agriculture lived in large villages, but had to move every ten to fifteen years when the soil had become exhausted and firewood depleted. In each village, the people had large, long rectangular houses, with a frame work of poles and a covering often of elm bark. Each "long house" sheltered a number of families. Such a village was enclosed within a stockade for defensive purposes. Non-agricultural groups had smaller houses, dome-shaped lodges, ridge-pole lodges and conical lodges.

During the winter, transportation was made feasible by snowshoes and toboggans. During the summer birchbark or elm bark canoes or dugouts were used. Yet water transport was not too important; overland travel was possible in much of the area. Clothing was made of hides, primarily that of deer, but in general was minimal, especially during the summer.

The Iroquoian people were organized into matrilineal clans (descent being from mother to her children). The women were the real social and political powers within such a community. It was they who elected the chiefs, who were males, and they could vote out of office any chief who displeased them.

The Algonkian people who lived in villages and practised agriculture had political organizations similar to that of the Iroquoians. The exception was that they were patrilineal societies. They possessed clans, in which inheritance was through the male line.

Warfare was an important component of life among the Indians of the Eastern Woodlands. Iroquois have been noted for their valour in battle and waged conflicts with most of their neighbours, extending their raids to the vicinity of James Bay and west to Lake Superior.

The Algonkians were as valiant warriors as the Iroquois. Their major endeavour was, after the defeat of the French in 1763, to oust the British from the Great Lakes. Under the leadership of Pontiac, they almost succeeded in this. There is no doubt that the military tactics employed by the Algonkians of this area were some of the best ever seen in North America.

The Indians of the Eastern Woodlands had a rich religion and mythology. Perhaps the two most prominent rituals were the Iroquoian *False-Face Society* and the Algonkian *Midewiwin.* The False-Face Society, composed of men and women, ritually cleansed the villages each spring and fall of illness and evil and cured those who were ill. Their main performance, though, was during the Mid-winter Ceremony, a series of rituals performed at the time of the new year.

Algonkian men and women who had gone through the appropriate initiations were members of the Midewiwin Society. There were eight degrees or grades through which one could pass. It was an organization devoted basically to the curing of illness among village members.

The Indians' Contribution to the European

The Indian peoples made a number of contributions to the Europeans. Perhaps the mo important were the many plants which the Indians had domesticated: maize, beans, squash, pumpkins, potatoes and tomatoes. Quinine and tobacco were other gifts.

Besides plants, the Indians had several item of equipment which the Europeans borrowe among them the birchbark canoe, snowshoe moccasin and toboggan. Lacrosse — both the game and the equipment used — was another item that the Indians originated and the Europeans adopted.

Furthermore, certain "loan words" such as *moose, toboggan,* and *moccasin,* not to mention all the place names derived from the Indian, were added to the English vocabulary.

Finally, the Indians provided geographical knowledge of the New World and guides to lead the explorers across the continent. In Canada, Matonobee guided Samuel Hearne across the barren grounds of Northern Canada in search of the copper mines of the Copper River, and Akaitcho guided Sir John Franklin on his first exploration through the Northwest Territories to the Arctic Ocean. There were many others whose names unfortunately were never recorded or have been temporarily lost in the archives.

The Europeans' Contribution to the Indians

With the coming of Europeans to the New World, the way of life of the Indians began to change and in time changed radically. The earliest alterations were brought about by trade goods, especially metal tools. These diffused rapidly from group to group, often before the Indians had met Europeans. And to obtain them, the Indian exchanged furs which caused other changes in his way of life. In some ways, the introduction of trade goods was beneficial in that it made the Indians' work easier. But at the same time, contact with Europeans was disastrous. A variety of diseases, especially smallpox against which the Indians had little or no resistance, soon began to sweep through the country, killing all ages by the thousands. Only recently has disease been successfully checked.

Another disturbing factor was the railroads. These forced the Indians to move from their lands. Railroads also made possible the more effective colonization of the southern part of Canada by farmers, who soon took over much of the lands held by the Indians. Furthermore, wildlife was needlessly slaughtered, such as the bison and passenger pigeon. This produced great hardship for the Indians and often brought starvation.

With these developments, the Indian was no longer able to be self-sufficient. Accordingly, the government entered into Treaties with the Indians by which they were assigned to Reserves. No longer were they free to travel their former lands securing their own livelihood. When this occurred, the Indians' way of life became disrupted and disorganized and the Indian dispirited. The low point in terms of numbers and general living conditions occurred about the turn of the present century. But with renewed interest on the part of the governments, both federal and provincial, the Indian has been cared for to a greater extent than ever before. He has been given greater educational opportunities, health measures have been introduced and housing and other government programs started in an attempt to better his lot. Although much is being done, more has to be done, especially in the education of Euro-Canadians, before the Indian can take his rightful place in Canadian society.

The Indian Today

At present, there are approximately 250,000 Treaty Indians and an estimated 200,000 non-Treaty individuals of Indian ancestry. The population today probably nearly equals what it was at the time of European contact.

Many of the Indians, both Treaty and non-Treaty, live on reserves assigned to them by the government. But more and more are moving away from the reserves either into nearby communities or to large urban centres where they are attempting to make a life for themselves. Some are attaining an advanced education so as to become lawyers, doctors, teachers, nurses, politicians, geologists, farmers and construction workers in high steel. Some have succeeded but a large proportion of them remain in the lower economic strata and often find it necessary to depend upon welfare, a condition they do not wish to endure. They no longer retain, nor can they, their old way of life, but they have, however, retained many of the basic values that their ancestors held. They now wish to establish an ethnic identity of their own and take their place in a multi-cultural society — Canada.

Bibliography

Cardinal, Harold/1969
The Unjust Society
Edmonton, M. E. Hurtig Ltd.

Driver, H. E./1961
Indians of North America
Chicago, University of Chicago Press

Gooderham, Kent/1969
I Am an Indian
Toronto, J. M. Dent and Sons

Jenness, Diamond/1960
The Indians of Canada (5th ed.)
Canada, National Museum
Bulletin 65

Josephy, A. M./1968
The Indian Heritage of America
New York, A. A. Knopf

Levine, Stuart and N. O. Lurie, eds./1968
The American Indian Today
Deland, Fla., Everett Edwards Inc.

Murdock, G. P./1969
Ethnographic Bibliography of North America
New Haven, Human Relations Area Files

Oswalt, W. H./1966
This Land Was Theirs
New York, John Wiley and Sons

Owen, R. D., J. J. F. Deetez and
A. D. Fisher, eds./1967
The North American Indians: a Sourcebook
New York, Macmillan

Steiner, Stanley/1968
The New Indian
New York, Harper & Row

Symington, Fraser/1969
The Canadian Indian
Toronto, McClelland and Stewart

Willey, G. R./1966
An Introduction to American Archaeology
Vol. I/*North and Middle America*
Englewood Cliffs, N.J., Prentice-Hall

Cover: Forehead mask inlaid with shell,
North West Coast. (ROM collections,
photograph by Arthur Williams)